ORDINARY
ZENSPIRATION

ORDINARY
ZENSPIRATION

FIND YOUR CHILL, FIND YOUR FUN, AND FIND YOURSELF

APRIL CACCIATORI

atmosphere press

Welcome to Ordinary Zenspiration...

Hello amazing You! Welcome to the little book that can:

Can create awareness.
Can change your mind.
Can challenge your ideas.
Can create new habits for you.
Can be fun.
Can remind you that ordinary is truly profound.

We all experience it, but what is it? Ordinary Zenspiration is a phenomenon that occurs consistently in our lives. The moments of pause and wonder that make up our days, weeks, and years, most so mundane and fleeting that they are taken for granted. These are the teaching moments that we often miss.

When I began paying close attention to the ordinary moments of my life, I discovered how blessed I really am. And it wasn't a moment of epiphany, more like a gradual awareness that grounded me in presence, alignment, and clarity.

November 1, 2015 was the date that a friend posted a "Gratitude Challenge" on Facebook, vowing to post one gratitude daily for the month. I felt compelled to do the same, and began my Gratitude practice that day. And didn't I feel a little twinge in my belly, wondering what my friends might think? Would they roll their eyes while reading my daily posts of gratitude, perhaps judging my authenticity, or even unfriend me because of my sudden positivity?

I mulled this over with the gremlins that live in the dark

recesses of my mind's Library of Scary Thoughts. Day after day, these gremlins and I conferred. That's how conditioned I was to 'dodging the proverbial bullet' and being über aware that the other shoe may drop. I was brought up believing that you were lucky if you got ahead in this world, and that most people were out to take you for a ride. Sharing good things was a bit too nice and ooooh, vulnerable. I would be a walking target for cyber bullies, to be judged for jumping on the happy train.

I decided it was my timeline and reading my page was optional. I mean c'mon, I'm sharing what I'm thankful for!

November 30, 2015 came, and I posted the last daily gratitude of the monthlong challenge. 30 days of gratitude and that was it? Appreciation for my life was to be shared in just 30 days? Hmmmmm. I knew there was something to this gratitude thing. I knew just 30 days of gratitude a year was a tiny, tiny drop in the big bucket of karmic existence. I knew I couldn't stop at just 30 days. Right then and there, I declared I would post my gratitude every day for the whole year!

Adding the sunrise photos was an obvious addition to my daily post. My backyard faces east. My nightshift life had become dayshift life and I was getting up around sunrise. I would wake facing an eastern window with the sun's entrance shining directly in my face. So many mornings I would open my eyes pre-sunrise and see the most amazing palette of colors and I would grab my phone and try to capture the beauty of it.

The extraordinary in the ordinary.

Of course, I had to share this too.
That year came and went, and I was still posting a daily gratitude. I recognized the gifts that were bestowed on me as a result of my practice. The gift of feeling grounded and present in this moment was, and still is, a really big deal. I felt my attitude shift into a more loving, non-judgmental view of

the people, places, and things around me. My family became even more precious to me. My massage practice deepened, each client again a sacred body on my table, and I am thankful to serve.

Most importantly, I learned to love myself unapologetically.

While developing new skills as a life coach, this daily gratitude practice grew more inspirational. Sometimes I would post a favorite quote, expanding on the deeper meaning. Most days I strive to share my own thoughts, concerns, vulnerabilities, and how I am moving forward. To this day, I'm still posting my daily Facebook post, sharing my core values, necessary boundaries, and the permission to do, be, and say the things that feel important.

As I added action steps to engage my audience, I was super excited to see that people were engaging. So many FB likes, loves, and comments! The responses were heartfelt, funny, even sassy; simple thoughts that provoke the profound. Friends and acquaintances were stopping me in the grocery to tell me how much they looked forward to my daily Facebook posts. Honestly, I was a bit taken aback. A daily inspiration that was affecting other people's day in a meaningful way?

I couldn't resist the calling to bring them together into this book.

Can I really change the world? Not without you!

How To Use This Book

I invite you to use this book as inspiration to get your Zen on and delve deeper into your heart and soul. We are so much more than what others think of us, so much more than we think of ourselves. Honestly, we are our own worst critics. It's time to shed the idea of who we think we should be and get on with just being. Allow the ordinary to show you the extraordinary.

Start on January 1 or open to any page for inspiration. Each Zenspiration is followed by an action step, encouraging you to move beyond your comfort zone, and experience the process of growth, for the magic truly does live there.

Here is a key of Action Steps:

Journal Prompt - A journal prompt means for you to create a written entry, expanding on your thoughts, with Exquisite Detail, and explore an idea deeper by physically writing on paper. Yes, in the book!

Exquisite Detail - Writing out thoughts and adding in detail encourages you to think beyond a quick answer and bring into view the things you would love to do, be, or see. This, too, is a practice; a place to build that muscle. An exercise in manifesting what you really want. Have you ever heard the saying: 'Be careful what you wish for'? It's true. Without clarity and the details right down to the exact make and model of that fancy car, you may get that Bentley, albeit match car size...

Visualization - Imagining people, places, and things in your mind's eye. This includes the sounds and feelings that correspond. Visualization helps you get to where you need to mentally. Remember that not all our work is happy work; some of it may feel uncomfortable, bringing up the darker side of ourselves. Trust that these feelings are not bad, but are expressing the need to be processed and felt.

Boundary Setting - Implementing boundaries to keep you safe and healthy. There are those that would consume all of you, your time, your energy, and anything else that would benefit them. Saying "No" without apology.

Values - Values represent what is important to you. Core values are what motivate your decisions and ideas of wrong and right.

Body-Mind Connection - Listen to your body. This includes Cultivating Quiet aka Mediation or the Quiet Sit that will allow you to hear your body. This allows you to trust your heart and gut feelings as the truth.

Dance Party - Get physical and move your body! Crank up your favorite dance music and dance. Feel the music vibrate through your whole body and move with it. Your heart rate increases, you breathe deeper, and the cobwebs or ruminations that have been holding you back are suddenly cleared away. How fantastic and refreshing a dance party for one is!

Personal Anecdotes - You will find short stories of my personal experiences strewn throughout the book.

Now you get to respond. To your heart, your intuition, to yourself. And BELIEVE that YOU are worth the time, the effort, the love. Get to know yourself on a deeper level. Get honest with yourself around the things that light you up and allow yourself to lovingly let go of the things that hold you back. The world we live in is abundant and infinite; it just requires your belief.

Ready, set, GO! I'm your biggest fan.
Love, April

January 1

So long last year, such a beautiful year of personal growth and much love shared with family and friends. I learned so much. How to celebrate the wins and take a loss and turn it into a lesson.

Hello New Year!

I love fresh starts, clean slates, and ooooh, the possibilities! Do you need help moving forward this year? Then please drop me a note, phone me, message me, I am your friend.

Who would you really love to work with this year? Who is going to help you reach those goals to attain that desired outcome?

And consider what gifts you might share with those very same people.

Journal Prompt:

List everyone you can think of and how that person will help you develop the skills, knowledge, or connections that move you forward. Thank them in advance for how they have already inspired you into action. In exquisite detail.
Then contact them personally and tell them.

January 3

Ah, the brilliance of some awakenings!
When was the last time you asked your body what it needs
before you got out of bed?
Then take the time to let it answer.
And really listen.

Body-Mind Connection:

Before getting out of bed, take a moment to ask your body
this question. *'Hey body, are you refreshed, stiff, hungry?
What do you need?'*

Then wait, observant to what surfaces. Listen. Respond with
care.

Honor your body. It is wiser than you.

January 7

There's something cathartic about cleaning out one's closet. Especially at the beginning of the new year. Out with the clothes no longer needed for whatever reason. Even that top that was such a steal, I couldn't believe the price and I just had to get it. And never wore it. The tags still sporting my retail win. Every time I tried it on, it just never looked that great on me. Not such a win. Thank you for the shopping experience, and now out you go!

To open yourself up for what is trying to come into your life, one needs to clear the way.

Body-Mind Connection:
Physically clearing one's space will clear the mind and heart. Prepare yourself mentally for the letting go and plan to get physical and move the stuff out.

Declutter. Toss it. File it. Donate it. Recycle it.

Personal Anecdote

Cleaning out my closet took 3 goes.

A little back story first. My closet was our closet. My family of 4. A walk-in that was packed to the hilt. Floor to ceiling boxes. Wall to wall clothes. Stuff precariously perched over other stuff. I wasn't even sure what was really there. Shared space because our little cape didn't have closets in the bedrooms. Nobody (me) cared about closets when we bought this perfect little house with the perfect country setting just a mile from town.

And 20 years later, we are considering moving. I better get a jump on the clean out. Hello closet for 4. So I go in. Sort of. I got in the first few inches and started pulling the obvious things that I could get to. I made a bit of space on the clothing bar to actually be able to move the hangers. Progress! 3 bags of clothing and some boxes cleared away. Phew.

Fast forward 8 months. I make another stab at it. Again, I venture in and go through what I think is doable. No to that shirt. Goodbye to anything under the size 'Mom of 2 kids'. Progress but not really the opening I had hoped for. Still better organized and I have a clue what is in the boxes.

Fast forward another year and we are now seriously looking for our next house. We know we are going to move within 6 months to a year.

This time I was mentally prepared. I had read up on the process of clearing the excess away. Every day, I would take a few things out. Thank it for its service, then decide which pile it should be disposed of in: 'Trash' or 'Donate.' I didn't have a lifetime for this exercise so I picked the day I would go into this clown car of a closet and empty it. Every last shoelace was coming out.

OMG, did we have a ton of clothes, shoes, boots, slippers, hats, and things.

Sort. Sort more. Bag it up. Decisions. Keep or go. Does it fit? What year is it from? Just say no to padded shoulders. The 80's are gone. You will never use the fabric from this piece for anything. Ever. Bag it. Keep moving. Call downstairs for backup! Please come get these bags so I have room to fill more.

And so it went. Each piece of clothing had to be something that was currently being worn. Not something I could fit into after losing 10 pounds. When that day comes, I get to shop for new clothes. I struggled with some of the things. I was emotionally attached. I asked myself, Is this something that will be part of my dream life? A yes meant back into the closet. A no meant it's out and which pile was appropriate?

The process was exhausting. After a shower, I realized how good I felt. Lighter. Clear headed and ready for the next steps. I was open for the next house to present itself to us. And it did. We moved into it 4 months later.

January 13

Happiness is an inside job. Listen to your heart.

Body-Mind Connection:
Cultivate Quiet aka Meditate.

This is the simple version.

Set your phone timer for 5 minutes. Sit comfortably with both feet on the floor. Take 3 deep breaths. Each one is released with an audible sigh. Next, close your eyes and simply breathe.

Say thank you to every distraction that comes in, and return to breath.

Say thank you to every distraction that comes in, and return to breath.

Say thank you to every distraction that comes in, and return to breath.

Then add another 5 minutes to your phone timer and begin again.

January 21

When I feel blah, out of sorts and in a bit of a funk, I like to crank up the tunes and my vibrations. Music is magic for the soul. To physically move the funk out, you gotta tap into your fave playlist and dance it out. I love how Pandora, Spotify, or Alexa will give you exactly what you need at that moment.

Dance Party:

What's your favorite dance party music? Oldies, Rock n' Roll, Pop, or Country, the point is this:
crank it up loud and move that body. Don't hold back.
Shake, rattle, and roll.

January 23

Imagine that every day gets to be a good hair day! Every day is simple, joyful, and easy. Ooooh, and you're not feeling it because you don't believe it's possible. You're feeling a teensy-weensy bit resentful and victimized.
Let's practice some gratitude today.

Journal Prompt:
List all the things you have to do. I have to _____. I have to go to work. I have to wash the dishes. I have to pick up groceries. Blah, right?

Now list the same things except replace 'I have to' with 'I get to.' I get to _____. I get to go to work. I get to wash the dishes. I get to pick up groceries. Ooooh, better, right?

One more step. List the same exact things and replace 'I get to' with 'I am blessed to _____.' I am blessed to go to work. I am blessed to wash the dishes. I am blessed to pick up groceries.

Ah. Feel the difference right there.
#Boom #Gratitude

February 2

Are you following someone else's path? "Be yourself. Everyone else is already taken." Thank you, Oscar Wilde, for the reminder. Great observation!

Take a real honest look at why you are doing the things you do. Is it because these are the things you 'should' be doing? Really? Who said so?

Journal Prompt:
What would you accomplish if you knew you would succeed?

No holds barred, let loose on this one. There is no failure, only wins. Write down all your 'shoulds'. I should work harder. I should take care of others. I should go to college and become a doctor because my parents said that's a great profession.

Continue writing in exquisite detail how and why you will give yourself permission to release those 'shoulds'.

Now you get to embrace the thing that really lights you up.

Bravo! Well done! Cheers!

February 9

The early hours of a crisp February morning before the sun rises. Sleep is never overrated. Look forward to slipping back into your dreams again... and sometimes your zone of inspiration is found after going right back to bed on a Monday morning.

Because you can.

Body-Mind Connection:
Snow days are random. Plan a Monday off just for you. This is extreme self-care and yes, you can. I give you permission to take Monday off. Or a Tuesday. Or a Wednesday...
#SnowDay #SelfCare

February 17

Q: Why is it ok to care for everyone else before you take the time for yourself?
A: It isn't.

Boundary Setting:

Practice saying NO. Without lengthy explanations. Without apology. I'm not available.

No, I can't.

February 29

Dare to live in technicolor. Be bold and wear the hot pink. Go ahead with a leap of faith that it will feel amazing because you know it will! You can choose the brightest color for your clothes, your walls, your pens, go for it.

My current brightest color is all things metallic in Sharpie pens. Ooooh yes, I loveLOVElove silver, gold, and rose gold pens for all these journal prompts! Often times writing with all the colors to emphasize important notes.

#NoRegrets #YesICan

Journal Prompt:
The brightest color for you is_____.
Why does this color make you feel _____?
Please write out beyond these tiny lines, in Exquisite Detail all the things you love about your brightest color.

Personal Anecdote

Dare to Take the Leap!

I was a shy, introverted child always on the edge of being aware of other's needs and feelings. I didn't understand how or why I felt these things and that it seemed others didn't. I had no idea that I was empathic and what that meant until I was an adult. Could I accommodate you? Should I get out of the way?

I practiced invisibility. Children were to be seen and not heard.

This affected my ability to lead effectively. Who could I lead and why would they follow me? So I became accomodating, doing what I should, never questioning the why or the order of things. No confrontation. Ever.

Until my late teen years. Actually I was in the 10th grade when I realized that only my opinion of myself was what mattered.

As freeing as that was, I still struggled to be authentically in-dependent. Seeking the counsel of others around many decisions in my life, and doing the things I should be doing based on what I thought was expected of me.

Heavy shit right there.

I ask you this: What would it feel like to not care, worry or fret about what others think you should be doing? How does it feel to choose the best and brightest for yourself, knowing that action isn't selfish, but self-ish? What would it look like to show up for yourself in a way that feels separate yet connected to those around you?

The Universe sees every single one of us as special, unique

and filled with abundant gifts to share. Gifts so valuable that not sharing them only holds us back.

I love to color, doodle and write with metallic sharpie pens and paints because it makes me shine. When I'm doing what I love, I can feel the shine that emanates from a heart overflowing with love. When your cup is overflowing, you can give more of yourself away.

It's time for that big leap with the brightest color that everyone will see!

March 10

Our words have the power to shift mindset, attitude, and outcomes. Oftentimes our most negative thoughts and words are reserved for ourselves.

Consider the words and phrases you tell yourself. You may not recognize them at first because they are used so frequently, it feels normal and ok.

"This is stupid. What was I thinking? I did it again. I'm not good with ____. I can't. It's too hard. What's the point? I'm a loser."

The truth is this, you are infinitely wiser than you allow yourself to be. You can figure it out. You can up the level of support for yourself by using words of kindness, love, and patience. Say Yes, for yourself. Every day. All day. Starting now.

Journal Prompt:
List all your amazing attributes in exquisite detail. Until you run out of ink!

Allow me to get you started:
I am a great listener, patiently allowing whoever is speaking

to complete their full sentence, listening to not just their words, but the way their body tells the story.

I can make a party happen with whatever I may have on hand in the pantry.

I know how to open wine.

I can grow tomatoes.

I'm a really great Mimi.

I can still deadlift at least 95 pounds.

I'm still learning.

March 14

Every day I take another step into the unknown.

Do you, really? Is that statement really the truth? Yes and No.

Unless you're psychic, the future is unknown, yet we take for granted the daily schedule we maintain. Think about it, everyday...wake up, bathroom, coffee, shower, work, home, dinner, bed. Many of us have no time for spontaneity, or time spent on nothing, enjoying the restful feeling of being idle.

Journal Prompt:
If you could wave a magic wand, what would you change about your life and why?

I say yes to Exquisite Detail here. True transformation requires clarity around the thing you desire.

March 16

"Told you so."
- sincerely, your intuition.

I'm not sure where I found that, but it makes me chuckle every time.

Mind-Body Connection & Journal Prompt:
How do you know when something is exactly right for you?

Where do you feel it in your body?

Describe this feeling in exquisite detail, my loves. All the juicy bits.

You'll thank me later.

March 30

Listening is more than hearing. When in a conversation, if you are already forming your response before the speaker finishes speaking, then you are not truly listening. You won't even really remember what was being said. People want to be heard. I know you do. To be heard, one must listen.

Body-Mind Connection:

Practice a deeper level of focused listening. That means getting quiet and no interrupting with your first response or shared experience until the speaker has spoken. Watch the speaker earnestly, how they hold themselves and the timbre of their voice.

You will discover that the speaker may have more to share than the words.

April 5

_____ is essential to my existence.

Journal Prompt:
What, where, and most importantly, why.
In exquisite detail!

Personal Anecdote

Love is essential to my existence.

Life without love would be empty, shallow, dark and lonely. At least that's what enters my mind first and foremost.

Love brings lush color and brilliant vision with a sense of belonging to the garden of life, intermingled with the people that inhabit this place. Love is inclusive. Love is infinite. Love fills my lungs with life and my soul with alignment. Love makes my heart burst. Love brings me to my knees. Love soars to the heavens.

I have a love for others. I have learned to love myself. I love the color yellow. Not exclusively I must add...for I love blue. All the blues. I love animals. I love nature. I especially love the ocean and the beautiful treasures that wash upon the shore. I love majestic mountains that make the sky seem even bigger.

Love is bigger than me and I love that.

Love is kind. Love is cruel. Love is all things.

Without love is to not exist.

April 17

Take more than a minute and imagine sitting next to a window that offers your favorite view.

Looking out on this vista makes me feel _____ because _____.

Visualization & Journal Prompt:

To imagine your favorite place and the view it offers can feel simple and easy. Take it a step further and describe, in exquisite detail, your particular view and how you feel while gazing at it.

How would it feel to be here every day? Why would you love this?

Personal Anecdote

My Favorite View

My favorite view is from the shade of a cluster of palm trees, seeing azure and turquoise water lapping up to the shore. A warm breeze caresses my face and body, I can taste the salt from the shore.

The rhythm of ocean waves calms my sense of feeling hurried, transforming time into timelessness. From this place I feel freedom and repose. I am able to dream without an agenda. Lazy love envelopes me.

Another view is from the back porch of my mountain cabin. Through the Tamarack Pines, I can see the smooth surface of the lake glistening and reflecting the tall trees that grow close to her shores. The scent of fresh balsam is everywhere while the morning mist is rising and a loon calls to their mate. I am rooted in time and space.

And I will keep these special places tucked into my mind's eye forever, ready to pull it forth anytime I need a minute of peace.

Any place that can evoke the sense of timelessness is extraordinary, for it allows you to move in the real time of love, not obligation.

April 23

There are amazing people in our world that surprise and delight, often when least expected, and for that I am grateful.

Body-Mind Connection:
Heart to hand.

Recognize those that have made a difference in your life with an old school handwritten thank you note.

Snail mail that comes from a friend is always a delight.

April 30

These mountains that you are carrying, you were only supposed to climb. -Najwa Zebian

I feel lighter knowing that I can set down heavy, worrisome burdens. That doesn't mean ignore, just that I don't have to bear the weight every moment. What are you carrying to the point of detriment?

Setting Boundaries:
Determine the thing that feels heavy, and then consider where you could let go of it or delegate the burden. This action places you in the position of receiving. Open your heart to receiving with gratitude, and say thank you. Do not reciprocate anything back to the giver other than your gratitude.

There is vulnerability around this and that may feel uncomfortable. Proceed anyways. Feel the feels.

Ask for help. From a trusted confidant. From a family member. Delegate to an employee or co-worker.

May 1

You can find me somewhere in between inspiring others, working on myself, dodging negativity, and slaying my goals.

Wanna play?

Journal Prompt:

Choose one of these or all three.

1. Describe your current self-care.
2. List 3 wins that you are excited about.
3. How are you inspiring others?

May 8

Ask me "Why?" and I will ask you "Why not?"

Why would I, should I, could I do this thing? We ask those questions of ourselves pretty often, I feel. And if it's not ourselves asking, it's a parent, spouse, sibling, or friend.
How does it feel to turn this question around and ask; Why wouldn't I, shouldn't I or couldn't I? Why not?

Your turn.

Journal Prompt:
There is a thing you keep questioning "Why?" Do you have a real and true "Why not?" Answer the above. Try the first thoughts that pop up and keep writing, in exquisite detail.

May 14

Each season brings an opportunity to transform ourselves. After the restorative rest of Winter, Spring arrives ready for tilling the soil and planting the seeds. We, like the earth, feel ready for new beginnings as Spring Fever creates the excitement necessary for action. It's time to plant your garden. What will you grow for yourself this year?

Journal Prompt:
If I were to move forward with one new project, what would that look like?

May 24

Personal Anecdote

I missed all the sunrises when I worked as a night shift bartender. Changing careers and moving to a day shift took some getting used to. Like, when do you get to the bank? I had no idea so many people grocery shopped between 4:30pm-6:30pm. Let me mention owning your own business. It's 24/7 accountability.

And we are capable of all things when it's a priority.

Making real changes in one's life takes resolve. It takes some chutzpah. As well as courage. Accountability.
And then there's the rewards.

Journal Prompt:
Prioritize your schedule. Ask yourself this: 'What is the best use of you?'

#dayplanner #trelloboard

June 2

You really can be yourself. Unapologetically. Because you are a badass!

It's not about fitting in.

It's totally about standing up for the things you know to be right and true.

It's about owning your thoughts, feelings, and ideas.

Unapologetically.

Authenticity requires vulnerability, transparency, and Integrity.

Journal Prompt:
List 10 core values, the things that really matter to you in life.

As we grow older, our values change. It's time to get clarity around what counts for you.

June 13

Life was meant for good friends and adventure!

Humans love being connected with each other and nature. There is a sense of belonging. And scientific evidence strongly suggests that this is psychologically essential to feeling fulfilled with your life.

Body-Mind Connection:
Road Trip. Somewhere. Near or far. Spontaneous or planned.

Take a drive to a local museum, park, or restaurant that sounds interesting. Do bring your loves, family, and/or friends!

June 27

What's one thing you would change about yourself?
Why?
What if that one thing is really your superpower?

Journal Prompt:
Write about the one thing you would change and why this change would be important.

To really know more, check in with a trusted friend. Have them honestly share your best attributes and shortcomings. You must be open to constructive criticism. Others see what we cannot. That includes our superpowers and our blind spots.

June 30

We have the ability to figure it out. This process is fueled by rest. For real. You are going to spin your wheels every time you find yourself working through exhaustion, overwhelm, and burn out. This is the worst time to push through something and soldier on.

Trust me. I had a long series of do-overs because I kept going in spite of myself. No bueno. 🤩

Body-Mind Connection:
Stop it. Step away. Take a break.

Give yourself permission to slow it down. Even 5 minutes of quiet breathing will feel restorative.

When you rest, refuel, and recover, you become more productive, more creative, and a nicer person to be around.

July 4

When I grow up, I'm going to be _____.

When I grow up, I'm going to be Jacques Cousteau. Remember him?

Yep, that's my 7-year-old self dreaming about the ocean, deep sea diving and the Great Barrier Reef. And then I was introduced to FEAR. You'll get eaten by a shark. Also I got to meet LACK. There's no money in research.

Journal Prompt:
Fill in the blank as though your seven-year-old self were dreaming aloud with eyes wide with wonder. AKA Exquisite detail.

July 15

Ever tell a story about some crazy escapades that happened, and your listener stares back at you in disbelief? So, you follow up with "you had to be there." Yeah, that kind of story.

Tell me one of yours.

Journal Prompt:

Recall and write down a story that describes something unbelievable you did. Why yes, yes, I do expect you to write with exquisite detail, because after all, you do want me to believe you.

July 20

The only constant is change and to respond to change we use our greatest power: the power to choose.

I can choose to respond in any way I wish. I may even react with an emotional feeling I wasn't expecting. It still comes back to the choices you make.

How will I move forward? By choosing.

How will you move forward? By choosing.

Body-Mind Connection:
Lean into your decision-making process. Are you quick and decisive, or slower like a researcher, needing to know more?

OR are you unsure and feeling anxious that you may be making the wrong decision?

Practice listening to your body. You will feel the yes in your heart and the no in your gut.

July 27

What if? Why not?

Humans are hardwired for safety. It's in our neural pathways to avoid the charging tiger and imminent death. And in today's world there are tigers everywhere. Or so we think. Fear of failure holds us back more than one may realize. Our brains are sneaky in the ways we stop or limit ourselves. We can make ourselves physically ill, create addictions that numb, procrastinate and paralyze the forward movement. The fear of success sounds like BS, but consider how success would change yourself and how others may perceive you.

Journal Prompt:
What if I failed?
What if I succeeded?

What if_____, and why not?

Keep writing in some impressive exquisite detail until you've exhausted your possibilities.

August 5

Even when my eyes appear to be wide open to discovery and possibilities, there is always another viewpoint that can alter my way of looking at it.

Am I really seeing the whole picture?

Be curious. Consider another way, and that there is no wrong or right way.

Perspective is a concept unique to each person.

Visualization:
Practicing visualization techniques will sharpen your awareness of the people, places, and things you encounter as well as build new neural pathways in your brain by activating the creative subconscious.

Imagine a scenario you know well. A recurring family dinner perhaps. Bring up all the details you can think of. Who is there, what foods are on the table, etc. You know it well and you can actually hear the conversation that is taking place. You know who is going for the spicy food and who avoids it. You know who has soda to drink and you know who goes for the wine.
Now change seats and imagine this same dinner through the

eyes of another family member. The perspective shifts dramatically.

A child that can barely see over the table and doesn't quite understand the adult conversation.

The grandma that struggles to hear what is being said.

August 11

How does perfectionism show up in your life?
With everything perfectly in place.

I always thought I was more of a Type B personality because I'm pretty laid back, with the exception of these weird little quirks:

-Folding the towels a certain way.
-Stacking the spoons in the drawer.
-Working on a project until it was so overworked I was exhausted and bored from it.

I realized I held this expectation of others.

What motivates this set of standards? Is it self-judgement, or concern of what others will think?

Journal Prompt:
This one gets a bit sticky. Do it anyway.

What are you afraid of?

In exquisite detail, write out your fears of failing, looking stupid, not being good enough, and yes, of success.

Personal Anecdote

Stacking Spoons

She said I must let go of control. I smiled as she said it. Like I understood. Like I would. Do that. Let go. Of Control. How did she know me? In that one-time chat we were just finishing.

Let go of control. Yes ma'am. I'm already on it, I lied.

And because I lie, to no one but me, I get another dose of tough love, self inflicted, naturally. The Universe delivers.

I hear you. I am listening. My body has warned me. After a few weeks of high fevers and headaches. Bells Palsy. 5 days in ICU. Really, I'm listening now. I haven't a choice.

What we need. To evolve. To move a step beyond. Beyond our tiny, insignificant fear that we made up. That if I let go, there will be a crash.

How? How do I let go of control and climb out of the hamster wheel of deceit? My integrity keeps my obligations on a backlit board I can always see. Responsibilities that nip at my heels. Should I turn away? Should I take my hand off the wheel? How can I let go of it? I am the driver of all the things.

Let go of control. Your life depends on this. I heard you, Marilyn. But please, send directions. I can't stop stacking the spoons in my flatware drawer.

August 15

What is the largest crowd you've ever been in? And how did it feel?

Journal Prompt:

Write with exquisite detail about your experience in the largest crowd ever.

Personal Anecdote

1979, Pittsburgh, PA, Three Rivers Stadium for a Bob Seger concert with my friend Lil. We were 18 and loved Bob Seger.

Three Rivers Stadium has a capacity to hold 59K people. My eyes just got wider. 59,000 people. And this show was packed. We had general admission tickets which meant the floor and a whole lot of jostling and moving to see the show, to actually see Bob Seger. Lil was taller than me and could see over many people. I was short and viewed a lot of heads and shoulders.

After the first set, the floor cleared while folks hit up the bathrooms and we got a brilliant idea. *Let's quick move up front and take our stand at the edge of the stage.* We held our spots come hell or high water! And the lights went down. The spotlights lit up the stage and there he was. Right in front of us. Bob Seger.

The music began. We high fived each other with grins as big as that stadium and the first wave of the crush came. I felt my smallness in a big way. I felt myself being pushed against the stage wall. Wood. I push back. I'm squished forward again. I look at Lil, fear now real as my lungs are squeezed and I can hardly breathe. I felt panic coming on and I waved wildly at Lil. *We must retreat, we gotta get out of here.* I could hardly move in any direction as I was pinned in place.

I grabbed Lil's hand and did the only thing that would work. I turned and started screaming, *I'm gonna puke, move it! I'm gonna puke, move it!* And people moved. The sea of bodies opened and we made it out. Back to a looser crowd of head and shoulders. I could breathe. We could dance. We would live to tell the story.

#YouHadToBeThere

August 23

Laughing lowers blood pressure, reduces stress hormones, and increases muscle flexion. It increases the circulation of antibodies in the bloodstream and makes us more resistant to infection.

What always makes you laugh?

Body-Mind Connection:
Funny memes on the internet. Watch a comedy. Can you tell a joke?

Plan an evening out at your local comedy club.

August 28

Will say, won't say, can't say. We all have a bucket of these. It's the 'can't say' that really messes with us, subconsciously.

Journal Prompt:
What is your 'can't say'?

Validate it by writing it out.

Normalize it by giving yourself permission to feel that way.

Then, let it go in any way that feels good to you: scribbling over the words, coloring over the words, shredding the words...

September 7

Today I will move slower. I will be in love with each moment I get to experience.

Body-Mind Connection:

Self awareness. Presence. Mindfulness.
Focus your awareness to be in the now. When you find your mind drifting to thoughts around the past or the future, pull yourself back to where you are at this moment. Practice! Practice! Practice!

September 13

What are you studying and learning? Leaning into deeper understanding perhaps...Or maybe you're reading a great novel and traveling to another time and place.

Journal Prompt:

What have you learned in your life that feels significant?
What else do you wish to know or learn?
In exquisite detail, per favore.

September 16

When someone tells me "no," it doesn't mean I can't do it. It simply means I can't do it with them.

How does that feel?

I have asked family and friends many times to be my companion for an upcoming event only to find myself without an escort. I went anyways. The first time I felt a bit of anxiety. The second time, meh, no big deal really. I know I would have really enjoyed their company, but going it alone caused me to work on my confidence muscle. I actually ended up introducing myself to more people on those occasions.

To go, do, or be all by yourself is to be courageous. Well done!

Body-Mind Connection:
Feel all the feels around this!

Go out alone. To the movies. For lunch. Or coffee, with your journal. Ooooh, I love a great coffee house that smells richly of the deep dark beans with ample seating for reading, writing, and enjoying your solitude amongst other humans.

September 25

Today, open your heart to the quiet space within. If even for just a few minutes. I feel like I was overthinking what felt important to share with you today.

My wind chime is faintly singing, and that always reminds me that the important things are simple, and often overlooked.

Body-Mind Connection:
Chimes reminder.

Set your phone alarm to chime like the wind chimes at different intervals throughout the day. When you hear this, it is a reminder to stop what you're doing for just a moment and ground yourself with the simplest act today.

Breathe.

Breathe deeply and slowly three times.

Check in with your body after, taking note of how you feel differently.

September 29

I love that so many of you share about the random acts of kindness you receive, witness, or initiate.

I'm wondering how it would be to receive a deliberate act of kindness for yourself, delivered from yourself?

Perhaps give yourself some extra time in the morning for journaling, ask someone to take over the task of something you just don't love to do, give yourself permission to rest more...

Journal Prompt:
Manifest self love.

Tell me, in exquisite detail, that one thing you would love more of for yourself.

October 7

Sunny autumn days feel sweet as a ripe apple picked fresh. I love blue October skies where you can smell and feel the crispness in the air, with the maple trees just beginning to change color.

Many of you live in warmer climes. Do you miss the turning of the leaves? What makes autumn special to you?

Journal Prompt:
Describe in exquisite detail all the things you love about autumn.

October 10

Feeling rushed and harried?

Stop. Just stop and breathe deeply. Remind yourself that rushing changes nothing. Accept time will pass regardless. Realize you are time. Make the necessary adjustments in your life so that you own time. It's a real thing.

Body-Mind Connection:
Slow down and focus on the task at hand. Check in with your body.

Are you feeling anxious about finishing quickly? Ask yourself, why?

October 20

"Goals. There's no telling what you can do when you get inspired by them. There's no telling what you can do when you believe in them. And there's no telling what will happen when you act upon them."—Jim Rohn

Goals require leadership, self-leadership. Self-awareness, self-management, focus on the present while the long-term goal stays on the horizon. And I will add, a guide, a mentor, who will support, and lead helps me maintain focus on my priorities. I have many guides in my life that I am thankful for, that includes family and friends.

Look back to January and consider the resolutions you may have made. Did you achieve your goal? Did you fall short? Was the goal too lofty or not really a goal you truly wanted? Where are you currently? Still aspiring or in the IDGAF mode?

Journal Prompt.
Bottom line: What do you want?

Let's get clear on the Yeses and Nos in your life. Write these out by drawing a line down the middle of your page, like a T. Left side is the Yes column and the right side is the No column.

Fill in the columns.

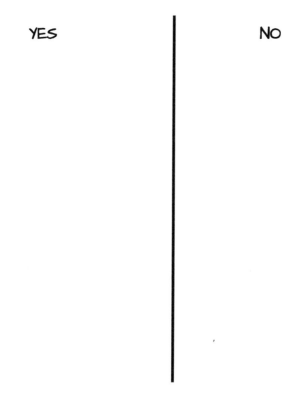

YES   NO

October 25

There are many times that you will not see the whole situation with clarity. Your brain assumes what you think you see is the truth.

So, when you begin to tell yourself a story around what you see, ask yourself if it's true and is there more to it...

Journal Prompt:

Write in exquisite detail a time you allowed a story in your mind to grow bigger than the truth, and the results of that action.

October 26

Trust your first instinct and just do it.

Body-Mind Connection:

Try something you have been holding back on. Feel into it. Go with your gut. You can fail your way to success. You will never know if you don't try.

October 28

Share a BIG brag about yourself today! Let's really pump up
the jam and show off. What's your superpower?

Me: I am really an amazing wellness coach!

Journal Prompt:
Your turn. Write down 20 brags in exquisite detail.

See how the sunrise brags.

November 11

Today I will _____ for myself.

Body-Mind Connection:

Today and this week, practice exemplary self-love and self-care. No cutting corners. #ItReallyIsAllAboutYou

November 19

It's harvest time. Celebrate the wins. Celebrate the seeds you planted, nurtured, and now reap. Assess the things that slowed you down, tripped you up, or got you stuck. Cool, when you let go of those, you've opened for a shift. A new thing, maybe not new...maybe it's a thing you have resisted in the past because it didn't make sense at the time. Or you denied it because it felt too hard, or you felt undeserving. Dig deep this morning. You can change the face of next year and it can begin now!

Damn! I'm excited for you

Journal Prompt:

5 Day Challenge.

Set aside 5 minutes each day for 5 days and describe 5 wins you have experienced thus far this year. Big wins and small wins.

Yes, you must write really fast, there's only 5 minutes!
Include 5 fails. We learn from the things that didn't go well.

They all count in the game of life!

November 22

Get your face to the sun and smile because you can!

Body-Mind Connection:

Smile big and wide at everyone you pass today. It's contagious!

November 27

Our greatest gift and power are the ability to choose. If only we humans really considered how to employ this superpower more often...how can you make great choices?

Values:

Choose one word to represent your intentions for the impending new year. This one word represents an intention that you wish to aspire to.

My first word was Creative, as I aspired to paint and create more. And I found myself in a conversation saying this, "If it doesn't nourish my mind, body and spirit, then it's out."

Whoa. Slow down there. Hold the phone. Creative wasn't my word after all.

My word is Nourish.

If there is ever a question around a thing I wish to do, be, or try, I will ask myself, "Will this nourish me, and how?"

December 12

The honest truth is this, there are some days I don't care to be in the company of others and their agendas. Call me selfish. Or self-ish.

And, when I get to that place, I get this ugly feeling. And I feel I mustn't say it out loud. The listener will not understand, and may be hurt or offended. What they don't get is that it's not all about them. It's all me. My feelings. My bottled-up-ness. My frustration. My overwhelm. My need to be alone, or on an adventure, even if it's only mental.

Body-Mind Connection:
Your body knows the feeling of retraction. We don't always name it. It's not pleasant so we push the feeling down and press on. Try feeling it. The message is clear.

Allow it. When you need to withdraw from the company of others, do so.

December 20

Through grace and a practice of mindfulness, we see that what appears to be ordinary, everyday, taken for granted, commonplace, and mundane is actually extraordinary.

Open your heart to give and receive and you will discover that every second you live and breathe, you are Ordinary Zenspiration.

Body-Mind Connection:
Sitting comfortably with both feet on the floor, breathe deeply and release an audible sigh. Thank yourself for this moment. Thank your heart for every beat, every time it showed you the truth, every ounce of love you have given and received. Hold the space for this exchange, it is not to be taken for granted.

Feeling into your alignment and love, repeat:
There's no place like home. There's no place like home. There's no place like home.

XOXOXOXOXOXOXOXOXOXOXOXOXOXO

Love, April

Sunrise over the Erie Canal, taken from the S. James Street Bridge, Rome, NY.

About Atmosphere Press

Atmosphere Press is an independent, full-service publisher for excellent books in all genres and for all audiences. Learn more about what we do at atmospherepress.com.

We encourage you to check out some of Atmosphere's latest releases, which are available at Amazon.com and via order from your local bookstore:

Tree One, a novel by Fred Caron
Connie Undone, a novel by Kristine Brown
The Enemy of Everything, poetry by Michael Jones
A Cage Called Freedom, a novel by Paul P.S. Berg
Giving Up the Ghost, essays by Tina Cabrera
Family Legends, Family Lies, nonfiction by Wendy Hoke
Shining in Infinity, a novel by Charles McIntyre
Buildings Without Murders, a novel by Dan Gutstein
What?! You Don't Want Children?: Understanding Rejection in the Childfree Lifestyle, nonfiction by Marcia Drut-Davis
Katastrophe: The Dramatic Actions of Kat Morgan, a young adult novel by Sylvia M. DeSantis
Peaceful Meridian: Sailing into War, Protesting at Home, nonfiction by David Rogers Jr.
The Stargazers, poetry by James McKee
SEED: A Jack and Lake Creek Book, a novel by Chris S. McGee
The Pretend Life, poetry by Michelle Brooks
The Testament, a novel by S. Lee Glick
Minnesota and Other Poems, poetry by Daniel N. Nelson
Southern. Gay. Teacher., nonfiction by Randy Fair
Mondegreen Monk, a novel by Jonathan Kumar

About the Author

April Cacciatori is a Body-Mind Coach, Massage Therapist, Owner of Zensations Massage Therapy, PLLC, Subscription Box Creator for The Zenspiration Box, Women's Retreat Leader, and author of *Ordinary Zenspiration, Find Your Chill, Find Your Fun, and Find Yourself.*

As a Body-Mind Coach incorporating her 15 year massage experience, April teaches the foundation of personal development and transformation through self-care, the deep listening to the body and mind intuitively with presence and awareness, while her multiple artistic energies compels the journey she facilitates for herself and her clients.

April and her husband Enzo reside in Rome, NY with daughter Jessica and family right down the street, and daughter Kelsey not too far away in Boston, MA.

CPSIA information can be obtained
at www.ICGtesting.com
Printed in the USA
LVHW010328240920
666824LV00006BA/523